A TREASURY OF

VETERINARY HUMOR

JOKES ABOUT ANIMALS, ANIMAL DOCTORS, ANIMAL CLINICS, & ANIMAL OWNERS

EDITED BY

SEYMOUR GLASOFER, D.V.M.

THE LINCOLN-HERNDON PRESS
818 S. Dirksen Parkway
Springfield, Illinois 62703

A Treasury of Veterinary Humor

Published by

The Lincoln-Herndon Press, Inc.
818 South Dirksen Parkway
Springfield, Illinois 62703
(217) 522-2732

Printed in the United States of America.

Library of Congress Cataloging-in-Publication Data

ISBN 0-942936-33-7
Library of Congress Catalogue Card Number 97-074590
First Printing

Typography by Spiro Affordable Graphic Services

To

Ronnie and Stan

For all the pleasure they have given

(including Mark, Scott, Joe, and Laura)

Preface

For more than fifteen years the column "D.V.M .*" (* Department of Veterinary Mirth) has appeared on the final page of each edition of *Veterinary Medicine/Small Animal Clinician* as a sweet dessert following the meal of continuing education for the practicing veterinarian.

Appreciation is extended to the editors of *VM/SAC* for permission to reprint many of the jokes that have appeared in this journal and sincere thanks is given to all the colleagues, D.V.M. and V.M.D., and friends who have supplied the author with all the bits of humor they have heard, read, or originated.

S.G.

TABLE OF CONTENTS

1
HORSE HAPPENINGS

"On the whole, your horse is progressing nicely," the veterinarian told the client. "His left hind leg is a bit swollen, but that doesn't really bother me."

"I guess you're right," replied the client. "If your leg was swollen, it wouldn't bother him, either."

Client: "That horse you checked for me is almost blind."
D.V.M.: "Well, I told you he is a fine horse, but he just didn't look good."

One of my clients says she bets on the horses just for the laughs. So far she has laughed away her bank account and her car.

Time brings about great changes. In the early days of this century people had horses and buggies; automobiles were playthings for the rich. Today everyone has an automobile and rich people move to the country and buy a horse.

An old farmer couldn't tell his two horses apart, so he cut the tail on one horse. That effort was useless because the tail grew right back. Trying another approach, the farmer cut the horse's mane, which also grew right back. Finally, he measured the horses and found that the black one was two inches taller than the white one.

After an accident a man was pulled from the smashed automobile and rushed to the nearest doctor's office.

"I'm afraid you're in the wrong office," the doctor said. "I'm a veterinarian."

"Work on me anyway," moaned the victim. "I was a jackass to try driving with such lousy brakes!"

The saloon doors swung open; a cowboy rushed out, took a running leap and landed in the street. Getting up, he brushed the dirt off himself and muttered, "Wait 'til I get my hands on the guy who moved my horse."

A fourth grader asked if it were true that a horse had six legs because his teacher told her class that a horse had fore legs in front and two behind.

A stubborn veterinarian and her equally stubborn husband had quarrelled and neither would budge when the phone rang. "I'm going out to treat a mule," she announced.

"Relative of yours?" he asked.

"Yes," she replied, "by marriage."

A baseball scout found a remarkable prospect—a horse who was a pretty good fielder and could hit the ball every time he was at bat. First time up, however, he slammed the ball into far left field and just stood there at the plate. "Run!" the manager screamed.

"Are you kidding?" said the horse. "If I could run, I'd be at the track!"

An old farmer was plowing with only one mule but kept shouting: "Giddap Hank, Giddap Boo, Giddap Jack." A passerby noticed this and asked: "How many names does that mule have?"

"Just one," answered the farmer, "but since he doesn't know his own strength, I put blinders on him and let him think a couple of other mules are helping him."

A farmer called his veterinarian to report that a horse he had just purchased would neither eat nor drink. "What do you think?" asked the farmer.

"I think," replied the veterinarian, "that if that horse is a good worker, you've got a bargain."

FRANKLY, I PREFER THE OLD FASIONED WAY

Client: "My horse keeps standing on three legs and scratching his stomach with his hind foot. What's wrong with him?"

Veterinarian: "There's nothing wrong with him. He's just feeling his oats."

CRCRCR

Mrs. Vet: "My husband puts in 16 hours a day—works like a horse."

Mrs. Client: "Why doesn't he take a vacation?"

Mrs. Vet: "Don't be silly. Whoever heard of a horse taking a vacation!"

CRCRCR

Did you ever hear about the thrifty cowboy who bought only one spur? He figured if he got one side of the horse to go, so would the other.

CRCRCR

"Mom!" cried the little city boy during his first visit to a dude ranch. "I just saw a man who makes horses. He had a horse nearly finished; he was just nailing on the feet!"

CRCRCR

A veterinarian walked into a blacksmith shop and picked up a horseshoe without realizing that it had just come from the forge. Dropping it, he put his burned hand into his pocket, trying to appear nonchalant.

"Hot, isn't it?" inquired the blacksmith.

"No," answered the veterinarian, "It just doesn't take me long to look at a horseshoe."

CRCRCR

4

The farmer who used to plow with a horse was not so bad off. No horse ever dropped $500 in value the minute the bill of sale was signed.

꧁꧂ ꧁꧂ ꧁꧂

D.V.M.:   "You're putting the saddle on backwards."
City Dude: "You think you're so smart. You don't even know which way I'm going to travel!"

꧁꧂ ꧁꧂ ꧁꧂

Student: "Is it correct to say I watered the horse when I gave it a drink?"
Teacher: "Yes."
Student: "In that case, I just milked the cat."

꧁꧂ ꧁꧂ ꧁꧂

D.V.M.: "Going to the horse races reminds me of my wife."
V.M.D.: "Why is that?"
D.V.M. "Oh, nag, nag, nag."

꧁꧂ ꧁꧂ ꧁꧂

I heard about a horse that accidentally shot himself; so they broke his leg.

꧁꧂ ꧁꧂ ꧁꧂

A veterinarian submitted a bill to a client as follows: "For curing your horse until it died."

꧁꧂ ꧁꧂ ꧁꧂

No man really realizes that a dog is his best friend until he has bet on a horse.

꧁꧂ ꧁꧂ ꧁꧂

"Could you take a look? She's a little horse."

CRCRCRCR

The owner of a very sick horse was told by the veterinarian that the animal would probably survive. "Will I be able to race him?" asked the distraught owner. "Oh yes," replied the veterinarian, "and you'll probably be able to beat him, too."

CRCRCRCR

Did you hear about the hermaphroditic horse that stood in its stall singing, "What kind of foal am I?"

CRCRCRCR

The blacksmith placed a horseshoe on the anvil and said to his assistant, "When I nod my head, you hit it." Funeral services are being held on Friday at 3:00 P.M.

Historians have traced the expression, "Hurrah for our side!" back to the crowds lining the streets when Lady Godiva rode side-saddled through Coventry.

CRURURU

Woman: "My husband thinks he's a horse, Doctor. Can you cure him?"

Psychiatrist: "I believe I can, but it will cost a great deal of money."

Woman: "Oh, money is no object. My husband just won the Preakness."

CRURURU

A veterinarian was called to treat a horse belonging to a notorious deadbeat who promised payment whether the doctor "killed him or cured him." The horse succumbed. Unable to collect his fee, the veterinarian took the client to court and explained the promise of payment. After considering the matter, the judge asked the doctor, "Since you did not cure the horse and you claimed you did not kill it, on just what contract are you trying to collect?"

CRURURU

Client to veterinarian: "Something is wrong with my horse. One day it limps and the next day it doesn't. What should I do?"

Veterinarian: "On the day that it doesn't limp, sell it!"

CRURURU

Thought for the month: It's inevitable that someone will create a successful fuel out of baloney and horse manure. After all, the politicians have been running our country on that combination for years.

CRURURU

A racehorse had won several races, but his owner decided to sell him. "He's a big ham," the owner told a prospective buyer. "He thinks he's in show business. The last time he came in on a photo finish, he turned so the camera would get his best side."

"That's alright," replied the buyer. "I'll take him anyway."

"Okay," said the ex-owner, turning to the horse when the deal was consummated, "This man is your new owner. Get up and do your lame impression."

CRCRCR

Horsepower was safer when only horses had it.

CRCRCR

D.V.M.: "My receptionist cried this morning at the sight of a horse with a broken leg."

V.M.D.: "She must be very sensitive."

D.V.M.: "No, this particular horse was in a box of animal crackers."

CRCRCR

Did you hear about the compulsive gambler who was continually losing all his money at the race track? He went to a psychiatrist and is now improved. He only goes to the track when it's open.

CRCRCR

My assistant's Mustang was recalled awhile back. Yesterday he got a letter from the Ford Motor Company saying simply, "Sorry, Podner, we had to shoot it."

CRCRCR

A farmer watching a veterinarian prepare to perform surgery on a young mule asked the doctor what she was injecting. "This is an anesthetic," the veterinarian replied. "After this, the mule won't know a thing."

"Save your money, Doc," replied the farmer. "That mule doesn't know anything now!"

🐎🐎🐎

The owner of a racehorse demanded to know why his jockey didn't ride his mount through a hole that opened up in the homestretch.

"Sir," replied the jockey, "Did you ever try to go through a hole that was going faster than you?"

🐎🐎🐎

A prospective buyer asked the price of a horse and was told $2,000. Gulping his astonishment, the buyer replied that he was prepared to pay only $200.

"That's all right," replied the seller, "I'll take it."

While counting out the money, the buyer asked why the seller had agreed to such a great come-down from the original price.

"Well," said the seller, "I just thought you said you'd like to own a $2,000 horse!"

🐎🐎🐎

A wealthy horse breeder offered a huge bequest to a veterinary college if the college would confer an honorary degree on his favorite horse. In need of money, the school accepted the offer, but the dean commented that it would be the first time he had ever been asked to give a degree to a whole horse.

🐎🐎🐎

D.V.M.: "Did the medicine I gave your horse straighten him out?"

Client: "Sure did! I buried him yesterday."

CRCRCR

Election years always remind us of the difference between a horse race and a political race. In a horse race, the entire horse wins.

CRCRCR

Veterinarian: "I see you have an eight-year-old horse entered into this maiden horse race. Why did you wait so long?"

Horse owner: "We couldn't catch him until he was seven."

CRCRCR

At a garden club meeting a nurseryman spoke on the advantage of using old horse manure for fertilizing spring gardens. One city-raised lady interrupted with a question, "You said old horse manure was the best fertilizer. Would you tell me how old the horse should be?"

CRCRCR

A farmer was having difficulty getting his new mule through the barn door because the ears were too high to fit through without touching; so he got a jack from the shed and started to jack up the barn when a neighbor came by. "What are you doing?" the neighbor queried.

"My mule won't fit through the door," said the farmer, "so I'm raising the door so it'll fit."

"Well," replied the neighbor, "why don't you dig a hole at the door so the mule can walk under it?"

"Because, " claimed the neighbor, "it's his ears that are too long, not his legs."

DaveCarpenter...

"GIVE IT TO ME STRAIGHT, DOC, HOW MUCH
LONGER 'TIL I'M EXTINCT."

II
CATTLE CALLS

"My associate is terribly forgetful," the older veterinarian complained. "It's terrible. I ask him to pick up a newspaper on his way back from lunch and he might not even remember to come back."

Just then, the associate rushed into the clinic. "Guess what!" he cried. "While I was at lunch I met the owner of the ranch north of town we've been trying to serve for years. Well, we got to talking and from now on we'll be doing all his veterinary work."

"See," sighed the senior veterinarian. "I knew he'd forget the newspaper!"

🐄🐖🐄🐖🐄🐖

Zeke: "How is your cow?"
Ike: "She died."
Zeke: "How long was she sick?"
Ike: "Just three or four days."
Zeke: "What ailed her?"
Ike: "Don't really know—she just got worse and died."
Zeke: "Who was the veterinarian?"
Ike: "She didn't have a veterinarian. She died a natural death."

🐄🐖🐄🐖🐄🐖

A new veterinarian in the area asked the rancher what he called his spread.

"Our family had quite a time picking a name," admitted the rancher, "so to please everyone, we call it the Lazy Rocker-Triple W-Diamond Bar-Lucky Sevens Ranch."

"Where are the cattle?" asked the veterinarian.

"There aren't any," was the reply. "None of them survived the branding."

Country gal: "You know, if you give a cow affection she'll give more milk."

City gal: "So what? So will the milkman!"

CRACRACRA

A farmer had been taken in so many times by the local car dealer that when the dealer wanted to buy a cow, the farmer priced it as follows:

Basic cow	$300
Two-tone extra	45
Extra stomachs	60
Product storage departments	60
Dispensing device (4 spigots @ $10 each)	40
Genuine cowhide upholstery	125
Dual horns	15
Automatic flyswatter	35
Total	$695

CRACRACRA

A boy and a girl were driving through the countryside when the boy stopped the car suddenly. In a nearby pasture were a cow and a bull amorously engaged. The boy put his arm about the girl's waist and whispered, "Boy! Would I like to do the same thing."

"Go right ahead," she said. "I'll wait in the car for you."

CRACRACRA

Have you heard about the livestock operator who named his place "Oleo Ranch" because it was a cheap spread?

CRACRACRA

A farmer's barn burned down and the insurance adjuster explained that his company would not pay cash but would replace it with another barn similar to the first. "In that case," fumed the farmer, "You can cancel the policy on my wife."

A pig was lamenting to a cow about how unpopular he was. "Everyone talks about your gentleness and kind eyes," said the pig. "You give milk and cream, but I give so much more—ham, bacon, bristles and my feet pickled, yet nobody likes me. I can't understand why."

The cow considered his question then answered, "Well, maybe it's because I give while I'm still living."

A tourist on a country road noticed a little girl leading a cow.

"Little girl," he asked, "where are you taking that cow?"

"To the bull," she said.

"Can't you father do it?" he asked.

"Nope," she replied, "only the bull."

The farmer's cow was a skinny, dried-up cross breed that no one would give $20 for—until she was hit by a train. Then her price went to $800.

Nature is amazing. Who would have thought of growing a flyswatter on the rear end of a cow?

A veterinarian's car stalled on a country road. When he got out to look under the hood a cow strolled over to him and commented, "Your trouble is probably with the carburetor."

Startled, the veterinarian ran to the nearest farmhouse and explained to the owner what had happened. "Was that a large cow with a brown spot over the left eye?" asked the farmer.

"Yes," replied the veterinarian.

"Well, don't pay any attention to her," said the farmer. "She doesn't know anything about cars."

We all know that when a bull is brought in to mate with a cow, that is called "serving the cow." So when we hear some politician say he wants to serve the public, we know exactly what he means.

An elderly veterinarian was losing his eyesight. In an effort to hide his failing vision from his younger associate he stuck a needle in a fence post. The next day when the two doctors were about 100 yards from the stock pen, the older one pointed to the post and said, "Isn't that a needle in that fence post?" But as he ran to retrieve the needle, he tripped over a cow.

Have you seen the new bumper sticker that reads "Eat fish today—make a steer happy?"

When a rancher complained to a veterinarian that his boots were too tight, the veterinarian suggested that the rancher have the boots stretched.

"Nothing doing," the rancher replied. "Every morning I've got to round up my cattle, mend the fences that have been torn down, worry about beef prices, watch my ranch blow away in the dust, and at night listen to my wife nag about moving to the city. When I get ready for bed and pull these boots off, that's the only real pleasure I get all day."

A journalism graduate got his first job as a reporter on a country weekly. The managing editor was very explicit in demanding that all details, including names, should be carried in every news item.

The first story handed in by the young reporter read "Last night during a severe electrical storm, lightning killed three cows on a farm south of town. Their names were Bossie, Susie, and Buttercup."

"Oh, what a lovely cow!" exclaimed the young miss from the city. "Why doesn't it have horns?"

"Well," explained the veterinarian, "Some cows don't have horns until late in life, others are born without them, and the horns are removed from some. This cow doesn't have horns because it's a horse."

The receptionist asked the veterinarian, "If your assistant had an accident with the practice car, would you rather he ruined the car or broke his leg?"

"That's a stupid question," answered the doctor. "Of course I'd prefer that the car was damaged."

"Well, then," said the receptionist, "I've good news for you."

A farmer who had an old, impotent bull bought a new, young, vigorous replacement. The new bull immediately started serving one cow after another. Watching this, the old bull began pawing the ground and snorting.

"You getting young ideas again?" asked one of the cows.

"No," replied the old bull. "I just don't want that young stud to think I'm one of you cows!"

A large animal practitioner, after being bogged down in a muddy road, paid a passing farmer $10 to pull him out with his tractor. Back on dry ground, the veterinarian remarked to the farmer, "At ten dollars a crack, I'd think you'd be busy pulling people out of the mud night and day."

"Wish I could," replied the farmer, "but at night I have to haul water for the hole."

A veterinarian was called to treat a bull that had been stabbed with a pitchfork.

The owner explained that the bull had attacked him and he'd used the pitchfork to defend himself.

"Why didn't you use the other end of the pitchfork?" asked the veterinarian.

"I would have," replied the farmer, "if I'd been attacked by the other end of the bull."

Farmer: "For the life of me, I can't understand why my black cows give more milk than my white cows."

Veterinarian: "Easy, it's because you've got more black cows than white cows."

An old bull and a young bull were carefully eyeing four young cows standing at the far corner of the pasture.

"Let's run down and make love to one of them," urged the young bull.

"Let's just walk down," calmly suggested the older animal, "and make love to all of them."

After paying my income tax this year I now know how a cow feels after milking time.

Have you heard about the nut who found some milk bottles in the grass? He thought he had discovered a cow's nest.

In Mexico, a man who throws the bull is called "matador." In the United States of America, he's called "Senator."

City Girl: "What a lovely brown cow."
Veterinarian: "It's a Jersey."
City Girl: "Oh, I thought it was its skin."

🐄🐂🐄🐂🐄🐂

Student: "What happens if you try to cross a Holstein bull and a Guernsey bull?"
Professor: "You get two very cross bulls."

🐄🐂🐄🐂🐄🐂

Teacher: "Name five things that contain milk."
Student: "Butter, cheese, ice cream, and two cows?"

🐄🐂🐄🐂🐄🐂

One large animal practitioner had been working much too hard. She woke up about 3 o'clock in the morning and her ear was ringing. She was so tired—she let it ring three times.

🐄🐂🐄🐂🐄🐂

The dairyman asked the veterinarian why he wasn't getting as much milk as he used to. "Guess you lost your pull," answered the practitioner.

🐄🐂🐄🐂🐄🐂

Thought for the times: If the price of beef goes any higher, India won't be the only country where cows are sacred.

🐄🐂🐄🐂🐄🐂

Scientists are planning to put 300 head of cattle into orbit. This will be the herd shot round the world.

🐄🐂🐄🐂🐄🐂

A veterinarian making a farm call came across a teen-ager whose car was stalled on an ice-slick road. He watched a moment as the kid took sand from the trunk and sprinkled it under the front wheels.

"Here, let me help," offered the veterinarian. "The sand should go under the back wheels."

Sneering at his stupidity, the boy replied haughtily: "The back wheels go around all right. It's the front wheels that won't turn!"

$$\text{🐕🐄🐕🐄🐕🐄}$$

A farmhand ambled up to the owner and commented, "Thought you'd like to know the bull's loose again and he's been chasing your wife around the pasture for the past half hour."

"You darn fool!" the farmer shouted. "Why did you wait so long to tell me?"

"What's the matter, Boss?" asked the farmhand. "Your wife short-winded?"

$$\text{🐕🐄🐕🐄🐕🐄}$$

A pompous government representative flashed his I.D. card and advised the old farmer that the card allowed him to look over the farm without interference. Shortly afterwards, the farmer heard the agent screaming for help and saw the farm bull in hot pursuit. "Show him your card! Show him your card!" shouted the farmer.

$$\text{🐕🐄🐕🐄🐕🐄}$$

A farmer was approached by a stranger and asked the value of his prize heifer. The farmer scratched his head and, after a contemplative pause, asked, "Are you the tax assessor or has she been hit by a train?"

$$\text{🐕🐄🐕🐄🐕🐄}$$

A newly married veterinarian was served some form of hamburger every night. When he sat down at the table he would ask, "How now, ground cow?"

One of our new country gentlemen wrote the county agent to ask "how long cows should be milked."
"Why, the same as short cows, of course," was the advisor's reply.

It's nice to be appreciated, or as the cow said to the farmer, "Thank you for a warm hand on a cold morning."

Politics is like milking a cow—you can get a lot with a little pull.

There was a rancher who had trouble keeping his hands away from his beautiful wife. He finally had to fire all of them.

Heard about the Wall Street tycoon who retired to the farm? He was an expert when it came to watering the stock.

When a physician friend of mine has a patient with a lack of faith in medical science he explains that a cow has no faith in the veterinarian, but he cures her just the same.

A farmer anxious to protect "Old Bossy" during the hunting season lettered C-O-W on her sides. The animal had no problems while the hunters were around but the farm tractor was riddled with shots. This could have been because on its side was printed D-E-E-R-E.

A young reporter ran into the newsroom of the Washington newspaper shouting: "Stop the presses! I've got the story of the year!"

"What happened," snickered the editor, "did a man bite a dog?"

"No," replied the reporter. "The bull threw a congressman."

CRCRCR

Sunday School teacher: "Who was unhappy when the prodigal son returned home?"

Student: "The fatted calf?"

CRCRCR

D.V.M.: "Your bull chased me yesterday and I had to leap up and grab the limb on the oak tree in the middle of the pasture."

Farmer: "That limb is 15 feet off the ground! How did you catch it?"

D.V.M.: "Oh, I missed it on the way up, but I caught it on the way down."

CRCRCR

I'M A

~~VETINARIAN~~

~~VETANARIAN~~

~~VETERNARIAN~~

DOG DOCTOR

24

III
DOGGIE DOINGS

One veterinarian has a sign on her wall: "The next time you call your dog a dumb animal, remember who he's got working to support him."

I once got a dog for my kid. It was the best trade I ever made.

Did you know dog catchers are paid by the pound?

One client had 3 puppies for sale and named them "Teenie," "Meanie," and "Paderewski." "Teenie" was the teeniest, "Meanie" was the meaniest, and "Paderewski" was the pianist.

"I've got a dog worth $500."
"My goodness, how could a dog save so much money?"

We all know how Columbus sailed for months and months and saw only water. Then, one day he looked out and saw trees. If you think Columbus was glad, you should have seen his dog.

Client: "Got anything to cure fleas on a dog?"
D.V.M.: "Don't know. What's wrong with the fleas?"

🐕🐕🐕

The man answered his doorbell and admitted a friend followed by a huge dog. As the two men talked, the dog knocked over a lamp, jumped on the sofa and began chewing one of the cushions. The outraged householder, unable to contain himself, growled, "Can't you do something to make your dog behave?"

"My dog!" exclaimed the friend. "I thought it was *your* dog."

🐕🐕🐕

A man walked into a pet shop, pointed to a large dog and inquired, "How much is that big dog?"

"Fifty dollars," replied the proprietor.

"How much for that medium-sized dog?" asked the shopper.

"One hundred dollars."

"And the tiny dog?"

"That one's two hundred dollars."

"Well," mused the perplexed shopper, "how much if I don't buy any dog at all?"

🐕🐕🐕

My son's nervous chihuahua is never going to provide much protection. Whenever I yell "Attack!" the dog has one.

🐕🐕🐕

Client: "I'm going to make a million dollars by teaching my dog to talk."

D.V.M.: "No one will pay that much for a talking dog."

Client: "No, but I know some dog food companies that will pay that much to keep him quiet."

🐕🐕🐕

After we told a client we had used the hospital's German shepherd for a blood transfusion, the client asked if the dog was full-blooded German shepherd. "No," we explained, "right now he's about 500cc. short."

The dog is man's best friend—the woman his most expensive.

Did you hear about the absent-minded client who walked into his veterinarian's office carrying a leash? He couldn't remember whether he'd lost a dog or found a leash.

A client just reported that her new puppy is now eating solids—plastic toys, pencils, rubber bands, and carpets.

One of my clients has a bulldog so dumb, he says, that it got its faced pushed in chasing parked cars.

True Story: When a frantic client called to say that her purebred poodle had mated with a neighborhood mongrel, she was asked to bring the dog to the clinic for hormone shots. Very soon the door flew open and the client rushed in and handed the poodle to the receptionist. "My Suzette!" gasped the client. "I called you about her a few minutes ago."
"Oh, yes," said the receptionist. "Mismated?"
"Oh, no," replied the client. "Miss Dillingham."

"I did!"

Ad in Levelland, Texas, newspaper: "Lost or Stolen—Chihuahua dog answering to the name Chicko. Brilliant dog, certainly aware of national and world politics—he shakes all the time."

A man lost in a snowstorm was approached by a Saint Bernard carrying a keg of brandy under its neck. "Oh, great!" exclaimed the man. "Here comes man's best friend... and a dog, too."

A veterinarian had a dog so intelligent that he decided to send the animal away to school.

A year later, as soon as the dog walked through the door, the veterinarian called his staff together to witness the dog's remarkable intelligence. "Did you do well in school?" he asked the dog.

The dog nodded its head affirmatively.

"Did you study history?"

The dog shook its head disdainfully.

"Mathematics?"

Again a negative shake of the head.

"Foreign language?"

This time the dog nodded its head with enthusiasm.

"Ahhh," said the veterinarian. "Say something in a foreign language."

"Meow!" replied the dog proudly.

<hr />

Did you hear about the plastic surgeon who grafted new eyebrows on a man, using hair from the hind legs of a cocker spaniel? Now every time the patient passes a fire hydrant he looks surprised!

<hr />

Every dog has his day, but puppies have weak ends.

<hr />

"Madam," said the veterinarian gravely, "I'm afraid your puppy has a compound fracture."

"Please, Doctor," wailed the client, "explain in plain English. I don't know anything about arithmetic."

<hr />

The local canine obedience school awards its graduates a *barkalaureate* degree.

There is a new special diet for constipated dogs, but it's not selling well in New York City. Dog-owners there figure if your dog is constipated, why fool around with a good thing?

We recently hospitalized a dachshund that had been treated with 160 acupuncture needles for a spinal problem. Actually, the back problem was cured but every time the dog drank water it looked like a lawn sprinkler.

Have you heard about the poor dachshund that died? He met his end going around a tree.

A man told a marriage counselor, "When I was first married, I'd come home from a hard day at work and my dog would run around barking and my wife would bring me my slippers. Now, things have changed. When I come home, my dog brings my slippers and my wife barks at me."

"You have no reason to complain," advised the counselor. "You're still getting the same service."

I'll tell you how smart one of our patients is. You know how some dogs roll over and play dead? This dog calls the mortuary to make funeral arrangements.

A small boy looked longingly at his friend's dog. "My mom won't let me have a dog for my birthday," he said.

"Maybe you've got to use strategy," replied the friend. "Ask for a baby brother. You'll get the dog."

D.V.M.: "What kind of dog did you say this is?"
V.M.D.: "An entomologist."
D.V.M.: "An entomologist is a collector of rare insects."
V.M.D.: "Right."

CRLRLR

D.V.M.: "How in the world did you get this huge Saint Bernard into your tiny Volkswagen?"
Client: "Put him in when he was a puppy."

CRLRLR

Maybe we ought to strike a blow for men's lib. Who started that discriminatory bit that *diamonds* are a girl's best friend, but a *dog* is man's best friend?

CRLRLR

D.V.M.: "What results did you have with that dog you were treating for anemia?"
V.M.D.: "Oh, I loaded him with iron pills and iron injections."
D.V.M.: "Is he okay now?"
V.M.D.: "As long as he faces north!"

CRLRLR

Shopping list: biscuits, meat, hair oil, vitamins, snacks—all for the family dog.

CRLRLR

Small animal practitioner: "Do you have papers for your dog?"
Client: "Yes, all over the house."

CRLRLR

LOST

SMALL DOG.   BLIND RIGHT EYE.

LAME IN BACK LEGS.   TORN EAR.

SKIN SORES ON BACK.   HAS
DEEP COUGH.

ANSWERS TO "LUCKY"

CALL 5.5.5 - 1212

I keep my word. I once told a client, "If we don't operate on your dog, he'll die." The client refused surgery. Sure enough, 14 years later the dog died.

🐪🐪🐪

Distressed client on the phone: "My dog has swallowed a bottle of aspirin. What should I do?"
Weary D.V.M.: "How about giving him a headache?"

🐪🐪🐪

Little Susie's dog was run over and she mourned for days.
"Come now, Susie," said her father, "you didn't carry on like that when Grandma died."
"I know," cried Susie, "but I didn't raise Grandma from a pup."

🐪🐪🐪

Answer for clients who want to know why Dalmatians ride on fire trucks: It helps the firemen find the fire plugs.

🐪🐪🐪

First client: "Why did you choose Dr. B to operate on your dog?"
Second client: "I saw a sign on the door that said 'Dr. A—2 to 5; Dr. B—10 to 1.' So I figured Dr. B was giving the best odds."

🐪🐪🐪

Did you hear about the dog that whelped near the highway because the sign said "Fine for Littering?"

🐪🐪🐪

On the receptionist's day off, the veterinarian stuck his head into the reception room and asked, "Who's next?"

"My dog," one man answered. He then proceeded to explain in vulgar terms the site of the dog's problem.

The doctor yanked the man into the examination room and admonished him, "Don't ever use that kind of language in front of people in my reception room again! Just say the dog's ear is bothering him. Then you can give me the details when we get in here."

Two weeks later, the same client was in the reception room and the veterinarian asked: "What's the problem?"

"It's my dog's ear," answered the client. "He can't urinate out of it."

CRCRCR

Just when I think I'm finally beginning to understand clients I run across one who refuses to drink from the same glass as her husband, but kisses her dog on the lips.

CRCRCR

IV
PUSSYCAT PATTER

One day, a client who was fond of practical jokes sent his veterinarian a telegram collect. It read: "My cat is perfectly well." A week later the joker received a heavy parcel collect, on which he had to pay considerable charges. When he opened it, he found a large block of concrete bearing this message: "This is the weight your telegram lifted from my mind."

CRCRCR

True Story: A client picked up his cat after a long and costly illness. "Well, now I've got myself a $300 cat," he remarked.

"No," the veterinarian replied, "you've still got a $20 cat. He just had a $300 illness."

CRCRCR

When a little girl's kitten was run over by a car and was dead on arrival at the clinic, the veterinarian attempted to comfort the child by saying, "Try to understand, Honey, little Tabby has gone up to meet the Lord."

"Awe, c'mon, Doctor," chided the girl. "What would He want with a dead cat?"

CRCRCR

Sign on a bulletin board in a veterinary hospital: "Help an unwed mother. Take one of her kittens."

CRCRCR

A client told me how he once tried to get rid of a couple of cats. He put them in a box and walked out into the country for several miles to turn them loose. "Did you lose the cats?" I asked.

"Not exactly," he answered. "And if I hadn't followed them back I wouldn't have made it home!"

One veterinarian quoted his hospital rates for cats at $20 a weak purr.

For a gift that keeps on giving—give a mama cat.

"Bad kitty."

A man frantically phoned a physician and explained that his wife, who always slept with her mouth open, had a mouse caught in her throat. "I'll be right over," said the doctor, "In the meantime, try waving a piece of cheese in front of her mouth."

When the doctor arrived he found the husband holding a mackerel in front of his wife's face. "I told you to wave cheese," exclaimed the doctor. "Mice don't like fish."

"Yes, I know," came the answer, "But I've got to get the cat out first."

🐱🐫🐱🐫🐱🐫

In an attempt to emphasize pet-population control during his speech to a grade-school class, the veterinarian commented, "A single cat can have as many as 100 kittens."

One pupil in the back of the room raised her hand. "How many do the married cats have?" she asked.

🐱🐫🐱🐫🐱🐫

Heard about an old maid who died and left her cat $50,000? Her dog is contesting the will.

🐱🐫🐱🐫🐱🐫

Quack: "Yessir, I gave that constipated cat a pint of castor oil."

Impressed listener: "Did it work him?"

Quack: "It was so effective that the cat now has seven other cats working for him; 3 digging, 3 covering, and 1 looking for new territory!"

🐱🐫🐱🐫🐱🐫

I fed my cat cheese. Now he waits for a mouse with baited breath.

Have you heard about the tomcat that was called "All-American" because he averaged 50 yards each night?

CRLCRLCRL

Then there were the two old maids who opened a cathouse. The first day they sold eight cats.

CRLCRLCRL

A boy watching his dad bury a cat that had been hit by a car said, "It won't do any good. It won't grow."

CRLCRLCRL

Sign of inflation: Three years ago an eccentric client left his cat $12,000. Today the cat is broke.

CRLCRLCRL

"I'm sorry, Mr. Jones," advised the veterinarian. "Just because your mother-in-law says she won't stay in your house unless you get rid of the mice is not reason enough for me to perform euthanasia on your cat."

CRLCRLCRL

A child came by the veterinarian's office to see about adopting a cat. He overheard his father telling his mother that he smelled a rat.

CRLCRLCRL

Our tomcat has had the surgical operation common to its type but still persists in going out very other night. I think he's in demand as a consultant.

CRLCRLCRL

D.V.M.: "If I find it necessary to operate on your cat, will you have the money to pay for the operation?"

Client: "If I don't have the money, will you find the operation necessary?"

* * *

The veterinarian walked out of the operating room and with his eyes turned heavenward announced to the client, "I've done everything I can do for your cat. How it's up to HIM."

The client thought for a minute and then said, "When we're through, do I send my check to you or to HIM?"

* * *

A woman met a friend leaving the veterinary clinic. "Oh," she said, "I see you took my advice and brought your cat to Dr. Jones. What did he say when you told him you were a friend of mine?"

"He told me I'd have to pay in advance!"

* * *

A new client tells me that the last animal hospital he went to was so expensive that every time he took his cat there, his wallet was placed on the critical list.

* * *

Veterinarian: "I'm sorry you had to wait so long to see me."

Client: "That's okay, Doc, it's just that I thought you preferred treating my cat's ailment in its early stages."

* * *

Warn your clients not to be misled by those ads that say, "If your cat has worms, cut out this ad." Cutting out the ad has nothing to do with ridding the cat of worms.

"Just to make sure, I'd like him fixed twice."

I had a client who loved her cat so much that when it died, we had to break the news to her gently: We told her it was her husband.

V
STUDENTS AND SEMINARS

A colleague tells me that his son in veterinary school has a spark of genius but at this point the lad seems to be having a little ignition trouble.

Vet Student: "Professor, is there anything I can do to become better at taking patient histories?"
Professor: "Yes. There's one thing, and I'll be happy to teach it to you." This exchange was followed by a long silence, and then:
Vet Student: "I'm listening, Sir."
Professor: "See? You're learning already."

The veterinarian in the next town, who has a son in college, defines *college-bred* as the product of the flour of youth and the dough of old age.

At a recent veterinary convention a very long, very dull presentation prompted one member of the audience to whisper to another, "What follows this speaker?"
"Tomorrow," came the weary reply.

A practitioner of my acquaintance has a quick-thinking young veterinarian working for him. When my friend asked the young man how he managed to spend $100.00 a day for meals at the AVMA meeting in Philadelphia, the youngster shot back. "Easy! I skipped breakfast."

"This X-ray shows a bad fracture," explained the veterinary professor, pointing to the film.

"And what does a good fracture look like?" asked the student.

🐱🐶🐱🐶🐱🐶

An applicant for a veterinary assistant's position comments that he got his D.V.M. degree last June—and not a dollar too soon.

🐱🐶🐱🐶🐱🐶

"No those aren't my diplomas.
They're my regulations."

Vet Student: "Did I really deserve a zero on my research paper?"
Professor: "No, but it's the lowest grade I'm allowed to give!"

CRCRCR

Professor: "There are so many interruptions in this classroom I can't hear myself speak!"
Vet Student: "Don't worry. So far you haven't missed anything."

CRCRCR

We know of a new veterinary associate whose colleagues call him thermometer; he graduated with all the degrees but no brains.

CRCRCR

Some of the frequent speakers at veterinary programs can talk for hours on any subject. Then there are those who don't even need a subject.

CRCRCR

Veterinary Professor: "What would you do in the case of a horse eating poisonous plants?"
Veterinary Student: "Recommend a change of diet."

CRCRCR

A veterinary student performing his first necropsy came to the final question on the lab form, "Disposition of carcass?"—to which he replied, "Kind and gentle."

CRCRCR

While demonstrating an operation on the program at a national meeting, a famous veterinary surgeon was boasting, "I've done this operation so many times, I know just where every blood vessel is." Just then, an artery started to spurt profusely. "See," he continued, "There's one of them now!"

CRCRCR

Why does a veterinarian have to go to school for six to eight years to earn a degree, when a client with a horse can learn enough to question a veterinarian's opinion just by joining a saddle club or owning a horse for a few months?

CRCRCR

At our last state meeting, we had a speaker who held the audience in constant suspense—everyone kept wondering when he would stop.

CRCRCR

A friend who just got the bill for his cat's surgery says he knows now why vet surgeons wear masks.

CRCRCR

At a recent live demonstration of a surgical procedure, the eminent veterinary surgeon performing the operation turned to the audience in exasperation and asked, "Will the party who keeps saying 'oops' please leave?"

CRCRCR

"I'm pleased to meet you," said the veterinary student's father to the instructor. "My son took anatomy from you, you know."

"Actually," replied the instructor, "he was exposed to it, but it never took."

A vet student wrote home, "You call yourself a kind father, but you haven't sent me a check for a month."

The reply: "Haven't you ever heard of unremitting kindness?"

The most popular speaker at the last veterinary meeting we attended was the fellow who had to catch a plane in half an hour.

A stranger in town mistook the local insane asylum for the veterinary college. Realizing his mistake, he quipped to the guard: "I suppose there isn't really a lot of difference between them."

"Oh yes, there is," replied the guard. "In this place, you've got to show improvement before you can get out."

Economists say that with all the new credit cards, we are creating a cashless and checkless society. Nothing new about that—it's all we had while I was attending veterinary school.

A renowned professor at a veterinary school is often asked what is his favorite dog. His stock answer should not offend any breeder or dog-owner. "My favorite dog," he replies, "is the well-behaved dog."

Veterinarian: "I'm sorry, I can't take on another associate just now. There wouldn't be enough work to keep you busy."

Recent Vet Grad: "You'd be surprised how little it takes."

Not only did the speaker at a recent seminar have nothing to say, but we had to listen for an hour to discover it.

"Is that question giving you trouble?" asked the professor of the veterinary student taking an examination.

"No," replied the student. "The question's easy—it's the answer I'm struggling with."

"It's Winky, my hamster. He's been in there ever since I told him we were going to see the vet."

"I'm worried," the veterinary student told his advisor. "My father works day and night trying to make enough money to keep me in school, and my mother spends all her time doing my laundry and preparing packages of my favorite foods."
"So why are you worried?" asked the advisor.
"I'm afraid they might try to escape."

No wonder colleges are a reservoir of knowledge. The freshmen bring little in and the seniors don't take any away, so it just naturally accumulates.

A young veterinarian seeking a job was asked if he was in the top of his class. "Not exactly," he replied, "but I'm one of those who makes the top half possible."

🐕🐖🐕🐖🐕🐖

A veterinary professor used the honor system when he gave an exam. At the end of the exam he asked each student to write and sign an honesty pledge. One student wrote candidly, "I did not receive any help on this exam, and the Lord knows I couldn't *give* any!"

🐕🐖🐕🐖🐕🐖

A colleague who did not believe in continuing education was chastised by the state board for incompetence. "You'd think," commented a board member, "that after 24 years of experience he'd know better."

"You have that wrong," observed another member. "In his case he has had just one year of experience 24 times."

🐕🐖🐕🐖🐕🐖

The curvy coed in the tight sweater wiggled up to the professor after class and, in a sugary voice, murmured, "I'm afraid I didn't do very well on the test today, but I'll do *anything* to pass this course."

The professor raised an eyebrow. "Anything?"

"Yes," she whispered, "Anything."

"Then study," he said dryly.

🐕🐖🐕🐖🐕🐖

Heredity is what a man blames when his son in veterinary school gets straight A's.

🐕🐖🐕🐖🐕🐖

Veterinary schools are finally teaching students the art of communicating with clients. For example, after an examination, a long, slow, thoughtful nod means: "Your guess is as good as mine."

Did you hear about the student who graduated from veterinary school but flunked his state board examinations because he couldn't spell D.D.T.?

"No one at veterinary school likes me," complained the son to his mother. "The students hate me and so do the instructors. I want to stay home."

"You must go," insisted the mother. "You're not sick. You're 42 years old and school shouldn't upset you. Besides, you're the dean!"

Vet Student: "Do animals with this condition die very often?"

Professor: "No. Only once."

We know a veterinary student who was so bad at surgery that his classmates claimed he couldn't even open up a conversation.

Two men were discussing their collegiate offspring. "My son at medical school is getting smarter all the time," bragged one. "His letters are so technical they keep me running to the dictionary."

"You're lucky," complained the other. "My son is in veterinary school. His letters are easy to read, but they keep me running to the bank!"

A famous anatomist was seated next to a veterinary student who asked the learned man what he did for a living. "I study anatomy," the man replied.

"Gosh," commented the student. "I finished anatomy last year."

※ ※ ※

My wife packed for the last veterinary convention just like Noah. She took two of everything.

※ ※ ※

At a recent veterinary meeting held in Rome, one of our American veterinarians looking at some ancient ruins remarked, "Looks like Hell, doesn't it?"

A native who overheard this remark shrugged and exclaimed, "Those Americans. They've been everywhere."

※ ※ ※

Young Graduate: "I'm going to build a new animal hospital."

Old Practitioner: "Humph! Never heard of anyone building an old hospital."

※ ※ ※

One veterinarian went to the crap tables while attending the meeting in Las Vegas. He lost everything he brought with him except his cold.

※ ※ ※

Back visiting the old campus a while ago, a young man walked by me saying, "Call me a doctor! Call me a doctor!"

"Why," I asked. "Are you sick?"

"No," he answered. "I just graduated veterinary school."

One new graduate has informed me that he intends to specialize in dermatology. When asked his reasons, he replied, "There are three reasons: I'll never be bothered with night emergencies, my patients will never die, and they will be a long time getting well."

Taking some of the courses at the AAHA and AVMA meetings proves that a lecture is something that can make you feel numb at one end and dumb at the other.

VI
FURTHER FARM FUNNIES

Inquiring of a farmer client about his neighbor, I was told that the neighbor was "such a liar that his wife has to call the hogs."

A farmer met another in town and said, "Say, Luke, I've got a sow with the sniffles. What did you do for that one of yours that had them?"

"I gave her turpentine," answered Luke.

When they met a week later, the first farmer announced, "Luke, I gave my sow the turpentine like you said, but it killed her."

"Killed mine, too," replied Luke.

A hen and a hog were discussing how they could contribute to the anti-poverty program. The hen suggested, "Let's give poor families ham and eggs for breakfast."

"Wait!" answered the hog. "For you that's a contribution, but for me it's a commitment."

A veterinarian received a postcard from a farmer living back in the hills, stating: "Send worm medicine. If good, will send check."

The veterinarian wrote back: "Send check, If good, will send worm medicine."

DAVE CARPENTER...

"He might have a computer-virus -- he ate mine..."

During a lunch break at the Western States VMA meeting in Las Vegas, a practitioner was heard to comment: "According to the price of this ham sandwich, the pigs I just vaccinated are worth $2,800 each!"

A large animal practitioner tells me that one night while he was out on another matter, the farmer asked him to look at a sow in labor. During the evening the veterinarian went to the pen several times, and each time he shone his flashlight in the pen there was another pig in the litter. Rather amazed, the farmer finally asked, "Doc, do you think it's the light that's attracting them?"

A colleague had 17 head of swine to vaccinate and was shocked when the express company delivered 2,015 doses of vaccine. The reason became clear, however, when he recalled his telephone conversation with the distributor. "I should have known," he said, "when the new order-taker answered 'Yeth thir' to my request for enough vaccine for 2 sows and 15 pigs."

A client wants to know: If M.D.'s have to study Latin, do D.V.M.'s have to study pig Latin?

Q: "What did the veterinarian give the farmer for the pig's rash?"
A: "An oinkment."

Q: "How did the pig get to the roof of the barn?"
A: "The swine flu."

A note to the swine practitioner—when treating a sick pig, consider that he'll have to be killed to be cured.

When asked what her husband does for a living, the pretentious wife of a hog-raising client insisted on replying that he earns his income with a pen.

A young attorney working on his first case had been employed by a farmer to prosecute a veterinarian for the loss of 24 of the farmer's pigs. He wanted to impress the jury with the magnitude of the loss. "Twenty-four pigs! Twenty-four! Think of that! Twice the number in the jury box."

So that you will be aware of coming down with Swine Flu, the predominant symptoms are high fever, general achiness, and a desire to eat slop.

D.V.M: "If your pig was sick, why did you give him sugar?"
Farmer: "Haven't you heard of sugar-cured ham?"

"Is 'Ballpoint' really the name of your new boar?"
"No, that's just his pen name."

There are all kind of equal rights. Don't you feel the President should authorize production of vaccine to protect swine from human flu?

Thought for the month: At today's pork prices, "living high on the hog" is really living high.

CRCRCR

A man was sued by a duchess for defamation of character because he called her a pig. He was found guilty and fined. After receiving the verdict he questioned the judge and determined that although it was wrong to call a duchess a pig, it was not illegal to call a pig a duchess. The man then approached the duchess and said: "Good day, Duchess."

CRCRCR

While visiting in the Southland, a Yankee met a farmer accompanied by a drove of hogs and asked, "Where are you taking those hogs?"

"I'm turning them loose in the woods to feed on the acorns," said the farmer.

"Why, up north, to save time, we pen them up and feed them corn. This shortens the time it takes to get them ready for market," the Northerner answered.

"Oh," replied the Southerner, "what's time to a hog?"

CRCRCR

Q: "Why did the three little pigs leave home?"
A: "Their father was such an awful boar."

CRCRCR

Want an easy way to get rich? You buy 50 female hogs and 50 male deer and put them together. Then you will have 100 sows and bucks.

CRCRCR

My family owned the original garbage disposal—a pig in our back lot.

"WHATEVER SHE'S GOT, SHE'S GOT A DARN GOOD
CASE OF IT."

Farmer: "Doctor, this vaccine was outdated 6 months ago."
Doctor: "That's all right. I use it only on pigs that should
have been vaccinated six months ago."

D.V.M.: "What time do you go to work?"
Farmer: "I don't have to go to work. When I get up in the
morning, I'm surrounded by it."

A drug salesman told me about a new injection. When I
asked him, "What's in it?" He replied, "About $9.50 profit."

One shrewd colleague drops this note to some clients whose accounts are in arrears: "Just pay me half of what you offered to pay me when you thought your animal was dying."

CRCRCR

These fellows stealing livestock from ranches and farms are usually pretty slick. However, one fellow caught red-handed stealing pigs explained afterwards, "The sow squealed on me."

CRCRCR

Farm Youngster: "For 10 cents my little brother will imitate a chicken."
Veterinarian: "What will he do, cackle?"
Youngster: "Oh, nothing cheap like that. He'll eat a worm."

CRCRCR

As one old farmer said to me, "He doesn't like his neighbor because this man ignores him, and he can't stand ignorance."

CRCRCR

When we dispense here, we tell the client that if they are not satisfied, they can return the unused portion of the medicine and we'll return the unused portion of their money.

CRCRCR

A firm believer in seat belts, Dr. Zilch on a recent emergency call, sped into a farm yard, unbuckled his belt, stepped out of the car—and his pants fell down.

CRCRCR

After a farmer was able to get all his cattle, hogs, chickens, and goats into their pens he remarked, "Now I herd everything."

CRCRCR

Out in Idaho a poor sheepherder's wife, in an effort to economize, decided to dye some clothes a bright red. She was mixing a tubful of dye in her yard when a young lamb gamboling by spilled the tub on itself. About a week later a buyer spotted the lamb and thinking it was a new breed, bought the lamb at ten times its real value. The rumors of a new breed spread far, and soon orders for red lambs were coming from all over. The sheepherder and his wife obligingly dyed many lambs and sold them at a substantial profit.

In fact, The couple is known as the biggest lamb dyers in the whole state of Idaho.

CRCRCR

The trouble with dairy costs is that the milkmen are pulling for higher prices.

CRCRCR

A new farmer wrote the following to his county agent: "Dear Sir: Every morning when I go out to my chicken yard, I find several chickens cold and stiff with their feet in the air. What is the matter?"

The county agent's reply: "Dear Sir: Your chickens are dead."

CRCRCR

Did you hear about the research veterinarian who crossed a chicken with a racing form and got a hen that lays odds?

CRCRCR

On a very busy day a veterinarian got a call from a city slicker, who was starting a poultry farm and wanted to know how long he should leave the rooster with the hens.

"Just a minute," replied the veterinarian who was busy talking with a client.

"Thank you very much," said the caller and hung up.

🐐🐑🐐🐑🐐🐑

First Vet Student: "What did you do this past summer?"
Second Vet Student: "Worked on a ranch where they raised hornless goats."
First Vet Student: "But ..."
Second Vet Student: "There were no butts."

🐐🐑🐐🐑🐐🐑

Then there's the farmer's wife who dropped her birth control pill in the chicken yard. The hens laid empty shells.

🐐🐑🐐🐑🐐🐑

Did you realize that a chicken is the only thing you can eat before or after it is born?

🐐🐑🐐🐑🐐🐑

An avian practitioner told me about a client of hers with rotten luck. He invested in a 25,000 chicken farm and the rooster was gay.

🐐🐑🐐🐑🐐🐑

Did you ever stop and think that a chicken's life is ova before it starts?

🐐🐑🐐🐑🐐🐑

As the Nanny goat said to the Billy goat, "Don't kid me!"

Those veterinary students study about cattle but after school they stand around the drugstore and appraise the calves.

CRCRCR

A farmer stopped at the veterinarian's office and was given much advice about nutrition without being charged for it. Gratefully, he announced that he would send a turkey to the veterinarian the next week. When the farmer stopped at the office again a month later for more free advice, the veterinarian mentioned in passing that he had never received the turkey he'd been promised.

"Oh, I forgot to tell you," the farmer explained, "That turkey got well."

CRCRCR

Instructor: "If a group of cattle is called a herd and a group of chickens is called a flock, what is a group of camels called?"

"A carton," replied the student.

CRCRCR

This winter it was so cold in Kansas that they had to build fires under the cows before they could milk them. And last summer it was so hot in Texas tht they had to feed cracked ice to the hens to keep them from laying hardboiled eggs.

CRCRCR

The new birth control pill for goats is called "Stop Kidding."

CRCRCR

DAVE CARPENTER...

"When I said, 'feel free to call me,' I didn't
mean FREE, free. . ."

VII
THE SUFFERING STAFF

Kennelman: "I really have a way with animals. Notice how all the dogs and cats come up and lick my hands?"

Receptionist: "They wouldn't be so friendly if you learned to eat with a knife and fork!"

Applicant for kennel work: "Before I take this job, tell me, are the hours long?"

D.V.M.: "Nope. Just sixty minutes each."

When asked how she liked the veterinarian she worked for, a secretary remarked, "Oh, he isn't bad, but he is kind of bigoted. He thinks words can be spelled in only one way."

A veterinarian's kennelman imbibed a bit too heavily at night and phoned the doctor's house the next morning to say he was too ill to report for work.

"That's all right," said the doctor soothingly. "You just go back to bed and rest well today."

"You certainly were very easy with him," the doctor's wife commented.

"I know," said the doctor. "Just wait until he realizes this is his day off!"

Detective: "Can you describe your missing accountant?"

D.V.M.: "Yes. He's about six feet tall and at least six hundred dollars short!"

I asked a colleague how he acquired such an efficient staff. "It's my work incentive program," he said. "Everyone who works for me keeps five simple words in mind: *One mistake and you're fired!*"

CRCRCR

I have a very responsible kennelman. No matter what goes wrong, he's responsible. His brain is especially remarkable; it starts working the minute he gets up in the morning and doesn't stop until he reaches the clinic.

CRCRCR

There are now twice as many persons involved in clerical work in veterinary hospitals as there were 25 years ago. We still don't know what's going on, but we're getting it all down on paper.

CRCRCR

A hard-working and individualistic old veterinarian finally hired a recent veterinary graduate to assist him. One of the first things he asked the new assistant to do was to sweep out the ward.

"But I'm a college graduate!" protested the young man.
"Okay," replied the old veterinarian, "I'll show you how!"

CRCRCR

Kennel Technician: The new title for the fellow who brings the mop when one of your patients has an accident in the waiting room.

CRCRCR

"How much did this microscope cost?" asked the technician.

"That was $600," replied the veterinarian. The technician responded with a low whistle and asked the price of the X-ray machine.

"That piece of equipment," answered the veterinarian, "is worth four whistles!"

After spending his morning off hunting, the veterinarian returned to his office, commenting to his receptionist, "I didn't kill a thing today."

When his receptionist replied, "That's the first time that's happened in years," four clients got up and left the waiting room.

Kennelman: "Pardon, Sir, I think you're wanted on the phone."

D.V.M.: "You think? Don't you know?"

Kennelman: "Well, when I picked up the phone, the voice on the other end said, 'Hello. Is that you, you old scoundrel?'"

Wanted: Receptionist for busy small animal hospital. Must look like a girl, think like a man, act like a lady, and work like a horse.

🐾🐾🐾

A veterinarian was having difficulty in getting a new assistant to act on his own initiative. After he had been told to handle his assignments as he saw fit, the assistant called the veterinarian and asked, "Should I finish the work you gave me yesterday or should I go on to the new job?"

"Yes," answered the veterinarian and hung up.

In a few minutes the phone rang again, "Did you mean yes I should finish what I started yesterday, or yes I should start on the new work?"

"No," responded the veterinarian and hung up again.

🐾🐾🐾

The four-day week is nothing new in my practice. I already have a kennelman who works a four-day week. Only he comes in six days a week to do it.

🐾🐾🐾

What can you say when your receptionist announces: "Good news! You haven't been paying malpractice insurance premiums for all these years for nothing!"

🐾🐾🐾

Overheard in the operating room:
    A: "Someone's deodorant isn't working."
    B. "Can't be me. I don't use one."

🐾🐾🐾

D.V.M. interviewing applicant for receptionist's position: "Do you know how to handle very difficult clients?"

Applicant: "Yes, Sir. I know both ways."

D.V.M.: "Both ways?"

Applicant: "Yes. So they will come again or so they will go somewhere else."

We know one veterinarian who hires only married men because they don't get so upset when he yells at them.

A veterinarian interviewing a new secretary mentioned, "I hope you understand the importance of punctuation."

"Of course," replied the young lady brightly. "I always get to work on time."

I know of a veterinarian who fired an employee, telling him, "You've been like a son to me—rude, insolent and ungrateful."

The veterinarian's aide sent him a note reading, "I'm due for a raise. Let me know when it will become effective." In her next pay envelope she found a note attached to her paycheck. The note read, "Your pay increase will become effective the day you do."

D.V.M.: "You're late again! Can't you do anything on time?"

Aide: "Yes, sir. I bought a car on time."

The director of an animal hospital offered a $25 award for the best suggestion on how to save money. The first prize went to a brilliant young aide who suggested that, in the future, the next award should be reduced to $10.

🐑🐑🐑

The aides in my office don't really respect me. Yesterday I walked in on a couple of them during their coffee break and one of them said, "Cool it. Here come the D-O-C-T-O-R."

🐑🐑🐑

The receptionist was rather untidy about her office and knew it. During lunch break she mustered enough energy to do a thorough cleaning. That evening the veterinarian approached her desk and, in dismay, complained, "Where's the dust from here? I had an important phoned number written in it!"

🐑🐑🐑

Kennelman: "I have good news for you, Doctor."
D.V.M.: "What is it?"
Kennelman: "Remember the extra 5 bucks you promised me if I didn't foul things up in the ward today? Well, you get to keep your money."

🐑🐑🐑

The technician at a busy hospital prepares sutures for a dozen operations a day. "And that," says she, "takes a lot of guts!"

🐑🐑🐑

The new kennelman rushed into the veterinarian's office and asked if he could leave work for a half hour because his wife was going to have a baby. When he returned breathless some time later the doctor asked if it was a boy or a girl. "I don't know yet," he answered. "You know it takes nine months."

CRCRCR

Two kennelboys were working in front of the hospital when a funeral cortege went by. "I wonder who died," said the first.
The second kennelboy answered, "It's the one in the first car."

CRCRCR

My kennelman has a motto: "Don't just do something — stand there!"

CRCRCR

The census taker asked my receptionist, "How many people work here?"
Her answer was, "About half!"

CRCRCR

The other day I noticed my kennelman had wads of cotton taped to his ears. I asked him what happened. He said he was clipping a dog and the phone rang; but instead of picking up the phone he put the clipper to his ear. "That's terrible," I said. "What happened to the other ear?"
He said, "I had to call the doctor didn't I?"

CRCRCR

Dr. John Doe's new assistant says you've got to be a contortionist to get along with his boss. He wants you to keep your nose to the grindstone, your shoulder to the wheel, your feet on the ground, your ear to the track and your eyes on the future.

Veterinarian: "Can you type blood?"
Job applicant: "Sure! First you press the 'b' key, then the 'l' key and then the other letters!"

"He thought the saguaro cactus was a tree."

D.V.M.: "That new nurse at the clinic has tried to romance every doctor there."

V.M.D.: "Intern?"

D.V.M.: "No alphabetically."

＊＊＊＊＊＊

My new kennel attendant is not too bright. He wants to take "One-A-Day" vitamins but can't figure out how many to take.

＊＊＊＊＊＊

Kennelman: "The dog in cage number 14 just bit my hand."

D.V.M.: "Did you put anything on it?"

Kennelman: "No, he liked it the way it was."

＊＊＊＊＊＊

My employees get two vacations a year—one when they go away and the other when *I* go away.

＊＊＊＊＊＊

Those of us who are getting along in years can console ourselves that when we're too old to set a bad example for our younger colleagues, we can always start giving them advice.

＊＊＊＊＊＊

A colleague always seems to be on the golf course. "Doesn't all the golf interfere with your practice?" a friend asked. "Not at all," the veterinarian replied. "I never play at the clinic."

＊＊＊＊＊＊

The owner of a local supply house gave a veterinarian one day to pay his bill. The poor-pay doctor chose Thanksgiving Day.

Back in his hometown for the first time in 40 years, a retired veterinarian found himself short of cash and presented his annuity check for $375 to the teller at the local bank.

"Sorry, Sir," explained the teller, "but we can't cash this for you unless you know someone in town who can identify you."

And wouldn't you know, the only person in town who could remember the veterinarian was a cousin who had lent him $375 forty years ago when he left for veterinary school—and who had never been repaid.

🐫🐫🐫🐫

A certain veterinarian is an avid golfer, and his wife is equally devoted to auction sales. Both of them talk in their sleep. During a recent night their children heard the father shout, "Fore!" After which the mother shouted, "Four and a half!"

🐫🐫🐫🐫

A veterinarian consulted a psychiatrist who asked, among other questions, "Are you troubled by indecent thoughts?" This colleague thought for a moment before replying, "Well, no, Doctor. To be candid, I rather enjoy them."

🐫🐫🐫🐫

Attending an out-of-town meeting, the veterinarian wanted to take a gift home to his wife. He went to a ladieswear shop and asked for a gown in his wife's favorite color.

"Will that be small, medium, or large?" asked the salesgirl.

"Yes," answered the veterinarian, "In that order."

🐫🐫🐫🐫

A veterinarian we know has the reputation of being more concerned with his practice than with his wife. He recently installed some new equipment in his clinic and noticed a spot of dust on it. "Have you an old rag?" he asked his wife.

"Yes, dear," she answered sweetly, "but I'm wearing it."

CRCRCR

Show me a veterinarian with both feet on the ground, and I'll show you a doctor who has trouble putting on his trousers.

CRCRCR

VIII
CLINIC CHATTER

Receptionist: "Is your dog leashed?"
Client: "No, I own him outright."

🐕🐈🐕🐈🐕🐈

When I heard a colleague tell a very difficult client that he wished he had a hundred like her, I questioned his sincerity. "It's true," he said. "I do wish I had a hundred like her. The problem is, I have a thousand like her!"

🐕🐈🐕🐈🐕🐈

Veterinarian: "You've owed me this fee for more than a year, but I'll be a sport and meet you half way—I'll forget half of what you owe me."
Delinquent client: "That sounds fair enough—I'll forget the other half."

🐕🐈🐕🐈🐕🐈

Client: "Will the operation on my little Fifi be dangerous?"
D.V.M.: "There's nothing to worry about. You can't get a dangerous operation these days for less than $100."

🐕🐈🐕🐈🐕🐈

After some of my experiences with my clients' children, I'm about to recommend that my clients try something different this summer: send their dogs to camp and their kids to obedience school.

🐕🐈🐕🐈🐕🐈

Two disagreeable clients sat in the veterinarian's reception room. "Close that window!" said one, "before I die of pneumonia."

"Leave the window open," complained the other. "I'm about to suffocate!"

In desperation, the receptionist suggested to the doctor, "Let's leave the window open and get rid of the first one. Then we can close it and finish off the other one."

"——AND IF I WERE A DOG
I'D BE 420 YEARS OLD."

My receptionist once asked a client if she had an account with us. After being told that the client did not have an account, the receptionist ushered the woman into the examination room with the introduction, "Here is a no-account client to see you, Doctor."

🐱🐶🐱🐶🐱🐶

"I'm sorry," said the deadbeat. "I didn't bring the money to pay for that distemper vaccination."

"That's all right," answered the practitioner. "We'll write your name on the wall and you can pay the next time you come in."

"Oh, don't do that. Everyone who comes in will see it!"

"No they won't," replied the practitioner. "Your overcoat will be hanging over it."

🐱🐶🐱🐶🐱🐶

Phone call at 3 A.M.:
> Caller: "How much do you charge for a housecall?"
> D.V.M.: "Twenty dollars."
> Caller: "How much for an office visit?"
> D.V.M.: "Ten dollars."
> Caller: "I'll meet you at your office in half an hour."

🐱🐶🐱🐶🐱🐶

I am frequently tempted to ask some of my clients to put a leash on their children and let their pets run loose.

🐱🐶🐱🐶🐱🐶

Client: "Sorry, but I can't pay you this week."
D.V.M.: "But you told me that last week and the week before and the week before that."
Client: "Well, didn't I keep my word?"

🐱🐶🐱🐶🐱🐶

Doctor: "What was that last phone call about?"
Receptionist: "Somebody wanted to know if you make housecalls—whatever that means."

CRCRCR

While visiting a colleague I noticed he had redecorated with an expensive silk blind in the waiting room and complimented him. "Oh," he said, "My clients donated it to me."
"That's unusual," I admitted.
"Yes," he continued, "I put a little box in the reception room marked 'For the Blind,' and the clients paid for it."

CRCRCR

I've just come to an agreement with the Bank-Americard Co. I won't encourage charge accounts and they won't treat animals.

CRCRCR

D.V.M.: "How's your practice these days?"
V.M.D.: "Terrible! Even my clients who won't pay their bills have stopped coming to me."

CRCRCR

Sign seen in a veterinarian's reception room: "Try our easy payment plan: One hundred percent cash—nothing else to pay."

CRCRCR

A veterinarian saw Harry Jones, an annoying client, approaching. He didn't want to deal with him, so he asked his aide to handle the case.
After a time, he shouted into the examination room, "Has that old pest gone yet?"
With great presence of mind the aide replied, "Oh yes, Mr. Jones is here alone now."

80

Receptionist to caller on the telephone: "Of course the Doctor will consider a housecall. What time could you be at his house?"

⌂🐏 ⌂🐏 ⌂🐏

Receptionist: "Whom shall we notify in case of an emergency?"
Client: "Just notify any doctor who's not too busy."

⌂🐏 ⌂🐏 ⌂🐏

One pharmacist tells me drugs are so expensive he won't fill a prescription until he has checked to see if it has been signed by a doctor and OK'd by a bank.

⌂🐏 ⌂🐏 ⌂🐏

Then there was the veterinary surgeon who believed in discussing financial arrangements with his clients. "Madame, how would you like to pay for this operation?" he asked, "in a series of piddling little installments or in one staggering sum?"

⌂🐏 ⌂🐏 ⌂🐏

Have you noticed that some people can never admit there's something they don't know? A client recently asked me, "What's that contraption, Doctor?"
"It's a sphygmomanometer," I answered.
"Hmmm," the client mused. "That's what I thought it was."

⌂🐏 ⌂🐏 ⌂🐏

Client (on the phone): "The dog I brought in last night that was hit by a car, is he out of danger?"
Receptionist: "Yes, he is."
Client: "That's good."
Receptionist: "Not really. He died this morning."

"As I say, he's a friendly sort."

🐕🐾🐕🐾🐕🐾

A colleague of mine is so busy that by the time he gets to any patient in the waiting room, the animal has already contracted two new diseases.

🐕🐾🐕🐾🐕🐾

We know a very successful colleague whose clinic isn't very fancy. In fact, it's so old it's already paid for.

🐕🐾🐕🐾🐕🐾

A veterinarian of our acquaintance has named his fishing boat *Consultation*. Now when he gets a call during his afternoon off, his receptionist says, "The doctor is out on consultation."

Today's children look at things differently. After the young boy's dog died in surgery, the veterinarian tried to console him with, "Remember, big boys don't cry."

"I'm not going to cry," the youngster replied. "I'm going to sue."

🐕🐕🐕

Dog owner: "How much will you charge to look at my dog?"

D.V.M.: "Nothing."

Dog owner: "Well, what's wrong with her?"

D.V.M.: "Oh, the diagnosis is $10.00."

🐕🐕🐕

D.V.M.: "How many people work in your clinic?"

V.M.D.: "Unfortunately, only about half of them."

🐕🐕🐕

D.V.M. (answering the phone late at night): "Don't you know my hours are 2 to 5 p.m.?"

Client: "Yes, but the car that hit my dog didn't!"

🐕🐕🐕

The new veterinary clinic in our town is so modern they're even using drugs that haven't yet been written up in *Reader's Digest.*

🐕🐕🐕

Someday a client is going to tell me, "This dog is just like one of the family." And I'm going to ask, "Really? Which one?"

🐕🐕🐕

The veterinarian called the client to convey good news and bad news. "The bad news," he reported, "is that I amputated your dog's front leg by mistake. The good news is that the infection in your dog's back leg is healing."

🐪🐪🐪

A difficult client was trying the patience of the new associate veterinarian who was attempting not to lose her temper.

"Get the senior doctor," the client ordered, "He possibly has more sense than you do!"

"He sure does, Sir," answered the young veterinarian. "He left by the back door the minute he saw you walk in the office."

🐪🐪🐪

A specialist has his patients trained to get sick during office hours only. A general practitioner is likely to be called off of the golf course by clients any time.

🐪🐪🐪

D.V.M.: "Was that one of your prominent citizens? I noticed you were respectful and attentive to her."

V.M.D: "Yes, She's one of our early settlers."

D.V.M.: "Early settlers? Why, she's so young!"

V.M.D.: "True. By early settler I mean she pays her bills on the first of the month."

🐪🐪🐪

A client who had been sent a bill bearing the the note: "This bill is now one year old!" returned it with the following note: "Happy Birthday, bill!"

🐪🐪🐪

"Worse. It's a flea <u>circus</u>."

🐻🐾🐻🐾🐻🐾

A frantic mother led her 10-year-old son into the veterinarian's office.

"Can a boy of this age perform a hysterectomy on a cat?" she asked.

"Certainly not!" replied the veterinarian.

"See there," said the mother, turning to her son. "Now will you put it back!"

🐻🐾🐻🐾🐻🐾

When a veterinarian's clinic burned down, the insurance adjuster explained that his company would not pay cash but would replace the clinic with one of equal value.

"In that case," fumed the veterinarian, "you can cancel the policy on my wife!"

One of our colleagues is giving a dance for his employees. He says it will be worth the cost just to see the whole staff moving fast for a change.

CRCRCR

A veterinarian I know can turn any situation to his advantage. Recently, before leaving his office to help move a new Hammond organ into his church, he informed his receptionist to tell all callers that he was busy performing an organ transplant.

CRCRCR

One large animal practitioner's dispensing area is so cluttered he had a sign posted, "We've got it—if we can find it."

CRCRCR

Client: "Hello, is your daddy in?"
Vet's daughter: "No, he's in the surgery doing an ovariohysterectomy."
Client: "My, that's a big word for a little girl. Do you know what it means?"
Vet's daughter: "It means 70 bucks—that's what it means!"

CRCRCR

"THAT? OH, IT'S A CATNIP PATCH."

VIX
ZANY ZOO

A youth found a rabbit taking its last gasps. He rushed it to a veterinarian who took a bottle off the shelf and held it under the rabbit's nose. Within a few minutes the bunny revived and appeared normal.

"What was that?" asked the youth.

Came the modest answer: "Hare restorer!"

"What do you get when you cross an elephant with a fly?"

"A zipper that never forgets."

A man approached a parrot in a pet store and kept repeating: "Hello. Hello. Hello." Finally the parrot turned to him and said, "What's the matter? The line busy?"

Let's not criticize the M.D. that treats a man and charges an arm and a leg. I know a veterinarian that treated a fish and charged him a fin.

Why is it that a nation that can split the atom and send men to the moon has to depend on a groundhog to predict how long winter will last?

A client who spent his spare time teaching his bird to say dirty words was recently arrested for contributing to the delinquency of a mynah.

CRCRCR

A man took his homing pigeon to the veterinarian and was told by the doctor that the treatment would be completed the next day.

"I'll be out of town tomorrow, " the client replied. "Let me pay you now, and then when you've finished with the bird, you can just let it fly out the window."

CRCRCR

An elephant was drinking from a river when he spied a snapping turtle asleep on a log. He ambled over to the turtle and kicked it all the way across the river.

"Why did you do that?" asked the giraffe.

"Because," replied the elephant, "I recognize that turtle as the one that took a nip at my trunk fifty years ago."

"What a memory!" exclaimed the giraffe.

"Yep," replied the elephant modestly, "turtle recall."

CRCRCR

I heard about a surgeon specializing in animal-man transplants. In one patient he transplanted the heart of a lion, the lungs of an antelope and the kidneys of a chimpanzee. The only complaint is that this man now smells like a zoo.

CRCRCR

Some time ago the rook was in danger of extinction. To help this endangered species, the government established a sanctuary. The director of the sanctuary had to resign after a short time because he could no longer stand being asked, "Have you bred any good rooks lately?"

A man bought a canary that was guaranteed to be a good singer. A week later he returned it to the pet shop, complaining that the bird was lame.

"Well, what did you want?" asked the shopkeeper, "A singer or a dancer?"

CRCRCR

When the circus was in town a man thoughtfully approached the camels. Then he picked up a straw, placed it on a camel's back, and waited. Nothing happened. "Wrong straw," he muttered and walked away.

CRCRCR

I'm writing a book of reminders—for elephants who forget.

CRCRCR

There were three ostriches. Two of them heard a strange noise and buried their heads in the sand. The third ostrich looked around and said, "Where is everybody?"

CRCRCR

Did you know?—The prong-horned antelope can leap across a 30 foot ditch... providing that he's being very closely followed by another prong-horned antelope.

CRCRCR

A woman visiting a zoo looked intently at the hippopotamus and finally asked the zoo veterinarian, "Is this one male or female?"

"Madam," answered the veterinarian. "That should be of interest only to another hippopotamus."

CRCRCR

"I was sewing."

✦🦁✦🦁✦🦁

Zoo veterinarian: "Is it possible to fall in love with an elephant?"

Psychiatrist: "Of course not!"

Zoo veterinarian: "Then do you know anyone interested in buying a 22-inch engagement ring?"

✦🦁✦🦁✦🦁

Have you heard about the marine life veterinarian who was arrested? They found him transporting dolphins across the state line for immoral porpoises.

✦🦁✦🦁✦🦁

Dr. and Mrs. Vet stood outside the gorilla cage at the zoo for a long time, unaware that the ape was staring at Mrs. Vet and becoming sexually aroused. Suddenly the gorilla reached through the bars, pulled Mrs. Vet into the cage and began ripping off her clothes.

"What should I do?" she screamed to her husband.

"Do what you do with me," replied her husband. "Tell him you have a headache!"

A mountain lion came across a bull grazing. He attacked and killed the bull. After devouring a sizeable amount of meat he threw his head back and roared proclaiming his victory. The roaring attracted the rancher who spotted and felled the lion with a single shot. The moral of all this: When you are full of bull, be smart enough to keep your mouth shut.

Veterinary professor: "What do you give an elephant with diarrhea?"

Student: "Plenty of room!"

While visiting the zoo, a little girl asked her father, "Daddy, how do lions make love?"

"I don't know, Dear," he replied. "Most of my friends are Rotarians."

A drunk stumbled into a veterinarian's office and asked, "How tall is a penguin?"

"About two and half feet," said the doctor.

"Thank goodness!" exclaimed the drunk. "I thought I'd run over a nun."

A client tells me that his wife does great bird imitations. For instance, she watches him like a hawk.

🐫🐫🐫

A youth was advising his friend what to see at the zoo.

"There'll be a sign 'To the Tiger'—you'll like them; and another sign, 'To the Giraffes'—and they're very interesting. But don't pay attention to the sign 'To the Exit.' I've looked; they haven't got one."

🐫🐫🐫

A veterinarian performed multiple surgery on an owl—a tonsillectomy and a hemmorrhoidectomy. During the convalescent period that owl was unable to hoot worth a toot or toot worth a hoot.

🐫🐫🐫

Did you hear about the near-sighted penguin who wandered into a convent by mistake and had a nervous breakdown? He thought he had shrunk.

🐫🐫🐫

After the ark came to rest on Mount Ararat, all the animals left but two snakes. "I thought I told you to go forth and multiply!" exclaimed Noah.

"We can't," they replied. "We're adders."

🐫🐫🐫

"Can you tell me the difference between 'unlawful' and 'illegal'?" asked the teacher.

One little girl's hand shot up, and she answered, "Yes, 'unlawful' is when you do something the law doesn't allow, but 'illegal' is a sick bird."

Could you describe a pregnant rabbit as one with an ingrowin' hare?

CRCRCR

Two drunks noticed a bug on the sidewalk. The first drunk says, "A bug."
The other nods and says, "Ladybug."
The first drunk says, "You've got damn good eyesight!"

CRCRCR

If you crossed a canary with a male cat would you get a Peeping Tom? If you crossed a basset with a beagle would you get a bagel?

CRCRCR

Two lions escaped from the Washington Zoo and fled into the city. After several nights they met. One lion was starving, but the other was sleek and fat. "I haven't eaten since we escaped," complained the starved one.
"Then come with me," said the fat one. "I'm hiding in a government building and every day I eat a bureaucrat."
"Isn't that dangerous?" asked the other.
"Not at all," replied the fat one. "They're never missed!"

CRCRCR

A man visiting a pet shop noticed a parrot with a string tied to each leg.
"What are the strings for?" he asked.
"Pull one and see," the attendant said.
He pulled the string on the right leg and the parrot said, "Hello there." Then he pulled the string on the left leg and the parrot said, "Pleased to meet you."
"What would happen if I pulled both strings at once?" the man asked.
"I'd fall on my tail, you dummy!" croaked the parrot.

"MAYBE WE SHOULDN'T HAVE HAD HIM DECLAWED."

A friend who specializes in avian practice tells of being asked to treat a psychotic owl. All the bird would say was, "Why? Why?"

Question: "How do porcupines make love?"
Answer: "Very, very carefully."

CRCRCR

Did you hear about the lion who ate a priest, a minister and rabbi—and had an ecumenical movement?

CRCRCR

Have you heard about the father who took his son to the zoo? He wanted to make a trade.

CRCRCR

In the zoo of a nearby metropolitan area the oldest elephant died. When the zoo veterinarian noticed the extremely sad faces on three of the attendants, he tried to console them until one of the attendants disclosed the reason for the dejection. It seems they were the ones chosen to dig the grave.

CRCRCR

Have you heard about the ape that read the Bible and Darwin's *Origin of the Species*? He was trying to find out if he was his brother's keeper or his keeper's brother.

CRCRCR

X
VETERINARY VARIETY

A few years ago a colleague was in financial trouble and I helped him out.

"I'll never forget you," he promised.

And he didn't. He's in financial trouble again, and he just called me.

CRCRCR

A colleague tells me he doesn't much like the telephone in his car. He says he's getting worn out from running to the garage every time the phone rings.

CRCRCR

At a recent meeting I asked an old veterinarian if he still found practice as exciting as it used to be. "Look, son," he answered, "I'm seventy years old. *Nothing* is as exciting as it used to be!"

CRCRCR

A doctor of my acquaintance refers to his fees for acupuncture as pin money.

CRCRCR

1st D.V.M.: "In the six years we've had this partnership, you've never agreed with me on anything!"

2nd D.V.M.: "It's been *seven* years."

CRCRCR

WHEN VETS CHANGE CAREERS

🐾🐾🐾🐾🐾🐾

"Integrity and wisdom are essential to success in practice," the older veterinarian told the new associate. "By integrity, I mean when you promise a client something, you keep that promise even if we lose money."

"And what is wisdom?" inquired the new doctor.

"Not making such fool promises!"

🐾🐾🐾🐾🐾🐾

D.V.M.: "I've started practice on the theory that veterinary medicine had an opening for me."
V.M.D.: "And have you found it?"
D.V.M.: "Yep. I'm in the hole now."

Many veterinarians have a problem with their leisure time: They haven't yet figured out how to keep other people from using it.

A young lady who was debating marriage with a struggling young veterinarian consulted a fortune-teller. "If you marry this man," the fortune-teller intoned, "You'll be tired, lonely, and unhappy until you're forty."
"And then?" asked the anxious young lady.
"By that time, you'll be used to it."

When the ark came to rest on Mount Ararat, among the creatures that went forth to multiply were some very prolific antelopes. This leads to the familiar expression: "No gnus are good gnus."

D.V.M.: "How do you spend your income?"
V.M.D.: "About 50% for food, 30% for housing, 25% for clothing, 20% for recreation."
D.V.M.: "But that's 125%!"
V.M.D.: "You're telling me!"

An exhausted veterinarian was enjoying a much-needed vacation in Florida when he received a collect long-distance call from a colleague noted more for his verbosity than generosity.

"I'll accept the call only if it's paid for at the other end," the vacationer told the operator.

The colleague agreed, and after 30 minutes of discussing trivia, the vacationing veterinarian felt obliged to say, "I guess you realize this call is costing you a small fortune?"

"Not at all," replied the caller. "I'm phoning from your office."

CRCRCR

V.M.D.: "I've heard paper can be used to keep a person warm."

D.V.M.: "It sure can! I had a mortgage that kept me sweating for 20 years."

CRCRCR

A veterinarian is a someone who believes in calling a spayed a spayed.

CRCRCR

D.V.M.: "I've given up wine, women and song."
V.M.D.: "Your doctor recommend that?"
D.V.M.: "No—my accountant!"

CRCRCR

Not long ago many veterinarians charged a flat fee for certain procedures. In recent years, however, some practitioners have knocked the "l" out of flat.

CRCRCR

DoveCarpenter.

" THERE'S NOTHING WRONG WITH HER. SHE'S JUST
GIVING YOU THE **SILENT TREATMENT.** "

We know a veterinary partnership that attributes it success to the fact that Dr. A makes the small decisions and Dr. B makes the big ones. Dr. A decides, for example, on the need for remodeling, a new X-ray machine, etc., while Dr. B decides whether the by-laws of AVMA should be changed, how many veterinary schools our country needs, etc.

About the only thing two veterinarians can agree on is how much a third veterinarian is earning.

🐫 🐫 🐫

Two veterinarians were leaving a lengthy seminar when one remarked, "I'd like something tall, cold, and full of gin."

"Gosh," replied the other, "I didn't know you knew my wife."

🐫 🐫 🐫

V.M.D.: "So now you and your son are carrying on the practice together?"

D.V.M.: "Not exactly. I run the practice and my son does the carrying on."

🐫 🐫 🐫

D.V.M.: "My wife is always asking for money. Yesterday she wanted $200, the day before $100, and today she wanted $50."

V.M.D.: "Good heavens! What could she possibly do with all that money?"

D.V.M.: "I can't say. I never give her any."

🐫 🐫 🐫

The amount of sleep needed by the average veterinarian is about 10 minutes more.

🐫 🐫 🐫

There is a new doggie deodorant called "Vanish." It makes the dog disappear so no one knows where the smell is coming from. And for the harried veterinarian there is a new 23-hour deodorant; it gives him an hour to himself.

🐫 🐫 🐫

A drug salesman calling on a veterinarian announced that his brand of vaccines had great nutritional value: The more he sells, the better his family eats.

CRLCRLCRL

It's sure good to know that success hasn't changed Dr. X. Ten years ago I couldn't borrow $5.00 from him. Now that he has made a fortune, I still can't borrow $5.00 from him.

CRLCRLCRL

Thought for the month: Show me a veterinarian who shoots golf in the high 90's and I'll show you someone who's neglecting the game. Show me a veterinarian who shoots in the low 70's and I'll show you a doctor who's neglecting the practice.

CRLCRLCRL

An important business problem was discussed at a recent veterinary meeting: If a surgeon leaves a forceps in a patient, should it be charged to the client or deducted from the surgeon's income tax?

CRLCRLCRL

First D.V.M.: "The greatest veterinarian who ever lived was Dr. Huggins—brilliant, generous, humanitarian, broad-minded, yet he died with his talents unsuspected."
Second D.V.M.: "How did you find out about him?"
First D.V.M.: "I married his widow."

CRLCRLCRL

Old veterinarians never die. They just smell that way.

A good many large animal practitioners must feel they're in a priestly profession. They're usually called just in time to pronounce the last rites.

🐂🐏🐂🐏🐂🐏

A veterinarian I know recently told me that a business consultant charged so much for telling him how badly he was running his practice that he couldn't have afforded to pay the consultant even if he was doing so well he didn't need him.

🐂🐏🐂🐏🐂🐏

One of the little-touted benefits of practicing acupuncture is that, if you're called in the middle of the night, you can always tell the caller to stick two pins in the animal and call you in the morning.

🐂🐏🐂🐏🐂🐏

The veterinarian who can smile when everything goes wrong has an associate to blame it on.

🐂🐏🐂🐏🐂🐏

Our state association has provided its members with very inexpensive group insurance. Only one problem: it pays only if the entire group gets sick.

🐂🐏🐂🐏🐂🐏

A veterinarian tried for several months to collect an overdue bill without success. Finally he sent a tear-jerking letter with a picture of his little daughter and added, "This is the reason I need the money."

By return mail came a photo of a voluptuous young woman in a string bikini. It was captioned, "This is the reason I can't pay you."

A veterinarian was telling his wife of meeting a former classmate who seemed to be having problems with his practice. "He can't hire and keep competent help, his clients are difficult and demanding, his billing system is inefficient, and his practice isn't growing as fast as he anticipated," the veterinarian explained.

"What did you tell him?" asked his wife.

"Well, I told him how to select good employees, explained how I handle difficult clients, and how to use a computer service to keep his billing efficient."

"That was kind of you," his wife replied. "What did he say?"

"Nothing. We just said goodbye, he climbed into his private plane, and I caught a bus home."

V.M.D.: "The doctor put me on a high-protein diet—nothing but steak three times a day."

D.V.M.: "How much have you lost?"

V.M.D.: "$342 in three weeks!"

* * *

According to a recent survey, there will be a surplus of veterinarians in 10 years. If you think it's difficult now to get a tee-off time on Thursdays, think what it will be like in 2006.

* * *

I know a veterinarian who says that when he can't find any other diagnosis, he labels the problem a reaction to the antibiotic he prescribed. The only trouble is, it's sometimes hard to explain to the client why the animal stayed sick for three weeks after it got well.

* * *

The average veterinary practitioner has five senses: touch, taste, smell, sight, and hearing. The successful practitioner has two more: horse and common.

* * *

In veterinary medicine a practitioner knows something about everything; a specialist knows everything about something; and a technician knows everything.

* * *

Two young veterinarians were discussing how they achieved success. "Things were real tough for awhile," admitted one, "but I just rolled up my sleeves, pitched in, and borrowed another thousand dollars from my father-in-law."

* * *

A man called his veterinarian about a swelling in his dog's leg and was instructed by the veterinarian to apply heat to the leg.

"But, Doctor," objected the client, "my wife says cold packs are better for swelling."

"You tell your wife," answered the doctor, "my wife thinks heat is best!"

CRCRCR

Overheard at a convention social hour—
V.M.D.: "Do you drink?"
D.V.M.: "I never touch the stuff."
V.M.D.: "Good. Hold this glass until I tie my shoelace."

CRCRCR

A young veterinarian devoted much of his time to studying tax shelters, averaging income, etc. Confronting his older associate, he asked, "When you list only what comes in and what you pay out, how do you really know what profit your practice has produced?"

"Well," considered the senior doctor, "when I graduated 40 years ago, all I had was my diploma. Since then, my clinic and my home have been paid for, my kids have graduated from college, and my wife and I enjoy a new car every three years. If I subtract the cost of my diploma from all that, then I know what profit my practice has generated."

CRCRCR

A colleague tells me that he has had to raise his fees because all of his costs are rising: drugs, dog food, wages, equipment, green fees ....

CRCRCR

XI
PET POTPOURRI

A woman who was trying to teach her parrot to talk said "Good morning" to it every day for several months. The parrot said nothing.

One morning the woman walked by the bird without offering the usual greeting. The parrot eyed her coldly and said, "Hmm! What's the matter with you this morning?"

According to a recent study, the most common causes of embezzlement are slow horses and fast women.

A fellow went into an animal hospital and said, "Give me some flea powder." The receptionist asked, "Should I wrap it up?"

"No," answered the fellow. "I'll send the fleas down here to eat it."

After much complaining to a breeder about the price of purebred dogs, the prospective buyer was referred to a used cur dealer.

Teacher: "Some plants have the prefix 'dog' like dogwood and dog violet. Can you name another prefixed by dog?"

Student: "How about collie flower?"

Q. "Where do goose pimples come from?"
A. "Feeding candy to geese."

Thought for the month: Puppy love can often be the beginning of a dog's life.

A neighbor, nearing 65, has taken to chasing young ladies. When his wife was told about this she just shrugged and said, "Well, dogs chase cars!" Being questioned about her unusual answer she explained, "A dog chases cars but if he catches one, he can't drive."

That vet student is always bragging about having plenty of girls on a string but the one he was out with last night looked as if she belonged on the end of a leash.

-PLETCH-

A man driving through the country saw a sign that said "Hound Puppy For Sale." He stopped, looked over the pup and in bargaining commented, "The pup seems nice but his legs are too short."

The seller took the dog, set him down and replied: "I don't know why you say that, Mister. All four of them touch the ground."

🐕🐕🐕

Money may buy the dog but love makes the tail wag.

🐕🐕🐕

Sticker seen on a sports car bumper—"Stamp out large dogs."

🐕🐕🐕

"Did you say the dog was shot in the woods, Doctor?"
"No, I said he was shot in the lumbar region."

🐕🐕🐕

Animal behavior note: Often the easiest way to get a dog to stop begging at the table is to let him taste the food.

🐕🐕🐕

A proposed new TV series is about an Alaskan sled dog and an Idaho potato. It will be called "Husky and Starch."

🐕🐕🐕

At our clinic we tried bathing a dog with one of the new herbal shampoos. Now instead of fleas the dog has fruit files.

🐕🐕🐕

A small animal practitioner tells about a client whose Great Dane chases sports cars. The problem is that he brings them home and buries them.

🐕🐕🐕

Said the dog as she sat on the sandpaper, "Rrrrufff."

🐕🐕🐕

Bumper sticker: "Animals are kind to dumb people."

🐕🐕🐕

A colleague became exasperated with a penny-pinching woman who consulted him about acquiring a pet. After her constant harping that she wanted a pet that wouldn't eat much, the veterinarian was prompted to reply, "Why don't you buy a moth? All they eat are holes!"

🐕🐕🐕

A veterinarian received a call about a hunting accident. "Is the dog shot bad?"
"Doc," answered the caller, "did you ever hear of a dog that was shot good?"

🐕🐕🐕

I asked this client if he had taught his dog to beg. "Yeah," answered the client, "but he doesn't even bring home enough to pay for his dog food."

🐕🐕🐕

Owner of a boarding kennel: "Madam, I've lost your cat and would like to replace him."
Cat-owner: "Fine. Start in my pantry. I just saw a mouse in there."

DON'T GO IN THERE! IT'S FULL OF VETS!

The skinny, mangy old dog coughed, wheezed, trembled throughout the examination. "I'm afraid I can't do much for him." said the veterinarian as he concluded the examination.

"Why not? demanded the belligerent client. "What's wrong with him?"

"Let me put it this way, Ma'am," explained the doctor. "If this dog were a building he'd be condemned."

Computers will never be able to do all kinds of paper work. How good would a computer be at housebreaking a puppy?

A client brought in a sheep dog with a skin problem. He said he didn't think the dog had fleas—he thought it had moths.

Tip on how to handle an alligator: Hold the mouth closed with both of your hands, then just maintain the status quo until one of you starves to death.

Tomcat: "I could die for you."
Tabby Cat: "Yeah! How many times?"

Upon checking the contents of my dog's commercial food, his vitamin-mineral supplement, and his coat conditioners, I discovered he is eating better than I am.

As part of your local association's public relations effort, we have been giving talks to various groups of young people. To make a vivid illustration about first aid, one veterinarian asked a class, "If you saw a dog lying on the roadside wounded and bleeding, what would you do?"

After a long hush in the room, one thoughtful little girl broke the silence. "I think I'd throw up," she replied.

All the dogs I know can read. Whenever they see a sign on a fire hydrant that says "Wet Paint," they do.

In Sunday school the children were told, "Lot was told to take his wife and flee out of the city, but his wife looked back and was turned to salt."

A youngster raised his hand. "What happened to the flea?" he asked.

Epitaph on the tombstone of a rock musician's tabby: "Man, this cat is really gone!"

Client: "The cost of feeding my dogs has gotten so high I can hardly afford to buy dog food."

V.M.D.: "Maybe you ought to rent it."

A veterinarian determined to forget about practice when he goes on vacation won't even let his kids buy animal crackers.

A dog owner called a veterinarian at two o'clock in the morning and said, "Doc, I want you to make a house call. Now get out your pad and pencil and I'll tell you where to go." You know, he didn't have to. The veterinarian told him first.

CRACRACR

A veterinarian received a phone call at midnight from a distressed dog owner. "I'm sorry to disturb you," he said, "but I can't get my two little poodles apart."

"Why don't you try pouring some water over them?" the doctor suggested sleepily.

"I've already done that," replied the woman, "but they didn't pay any attention."

"Okay," said the vet resignedly, "put the receiver back on the phone. Then carry them over to the phone and I'll call you right back."

"Oh," the woman said doubtfully, "do you think that will separate them?"

"Well," replied the veterinarian, "it just worked for me."

CRACRACR

A new associate explained how he embarked on a veterinary career this way: "I was working as a kennelman and fell in love with the receptionist at the hospital where I was employed. I quit my job, and after seven years I got my degree and passed the licensing exams. In the meantime, the receptionist married someone else. Now I'm stuck with being a veterinarian."

CRACRACR

In light of all the publicity about acupuncture, I'm wondering: Is it the penicillin that has been curing my patients, or just the insertion of the needle?

"Thanks for letting us borrow your book . . .
sorry it's a little dog-eared."

A colleague in Washington, D.C. tells me he only treats
animals belonging to members of the Senate; he doesn't
want to make House calls.

One client insists her dog is not spoiled. She offers as proof that he is the only one in the household that doesn't have his own telephone.

🐾🐾🐾

One recent chilly day a woman brought to the clinic a toy Poodle wearing a knitted coat. She registered with the receptionist, took a seat and after glancing at the other animals in the room, was heard to say to her dog, "See! I told you you'd be the only one wearing a jacket!"

🐾🐾🐾

A dog swallowed a ping pong ball and was rushed to the veterinarian for surgery. The dog's owner insisted on watching the operation and became alarmed at the number of incisions the surgeon made as he cut here and there in a rather random manner.

"Why do you have to cut in so many places?" questioned the owner.

"Well," replied the surgeon, "that's the way the ball bounces."

🐾🐾🐾

An epidemic wiped out the entire canine population in an Alaskan city. The place became known as Dogless Fairbanks.

🐾🐾🐾

One client always has his dog with him wherever he goes. When he stops at a diner or place that does not prohibit dogs he brings the pup in and orders a hamburger for the dog while eating his own meal. This is not unusual but he does get some strange glances when he tells the waitress, "Separate checks, please."

A woman showed up in the veterinarian's office and requested every possible kind of test and service for her dog. When the veterinarian presented a very sizeable bill, the woman explained that she had no money to pay for it. The exasperated veterinarian asked why she had demanded all the services regardless of the cost. "Because," replied the indigent client in a huff, "where my dog is concerned, money is no object!"

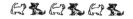

122

XII
DOC'S DICTIONARY

Adam: The only man who could relate a joke and not be told "Already heard it."

Agricultural Expert: Someone smart enough to tell others how to farm and too smart to do it himself.

Allergy: A diagnosis costing approximately $75.00 more than an itch.

Artificial Insemination: Inoculate conception.

Bank: Where you keep your money until the IRS asks for it.

Bargain: Anything selling for the same price as two years ago.

Bunnies: Rabbit's feat.

Buttress: A female goat.

Cadillac: A vehicle a doctor buys not to make house calls in.

Chimp-Pansy: A homosexual simian.

Class Reunion: Old friends getting together to see who's falling apart.

Conscience: What keeps you from enjoying sin.

Dermatologist: One who practices itchraft.

Doctor: A man who tells you if you don't cut out something, he'll cut out something.

Dogma: A bitch that has just whelped.

A dollar saved: A quarter earned.

Examination: The only time when what you don't know can hurt you.

Expert diagnostician: One who knows his diagnoses are always right because he has the necropsy reports to prove it.

Expletive: A nine-letter word that means a four-letter word.

Fat cat: A flabby tabby.

Frustration: Having no one to blame but yourself.

Gentleman farmer: A man who left the country to make enough money in the city so he could afford to live in the country.

George Washington Bridge: The First President's dentures.

Gossip: Letting the chat out of the bag.

Hangover: The wrath of grapes.

Impotence: Emission impossible.

Inflation: (1)   When you have money to burn but can't afford matches;
(2)   Being broke with a pocketful of money;
(3)   What makes an item you bought five

years ago for $10 now cost $15 to repair;

(4)   When half of your incomes goes for necessities—and so does the other half;

(5)   When the buck doesn't stop anywhere.

Living wage: Twice what you make.

Loveable: What a cow does for her sex life.

Loyal employee: One who covers for you when you're sick and puts up with you when you're well.

Lumpy jaw: A 6-year-old child with a nickle's worth of bubble gum.

Matched luggage: Two shopping bags from the same store.

Matrimonial dyspepsia: When your spouse doesn't agree with you.

Mayor: Female horse.

Mixed greens: Assortment of fives, tens, and twenties.

Model veterinarian: A small imitation of the real thing.

Octopus: An eight-sided cat.

Old-timer: Anyone who remembers when radioactivity meant static.

Paradox: Two veterinarians.

Peeping tom: A cross between a canary and a tomcat.

Pharmacist: A fellow who stands behind a soda fountain in a white coat and sells greeting cards.

Pink elephant: A beast of bourbon.

Politics: Parrot after it swallowed a watch.

Polyunsaturated: A dry parrot.

Pony: A compact horse.

Pregnancy: When a female can do nothing and still be productive.

Prescription: The only thing harder to read than the handwriting on the wall.

Primate: Sultan's favorite wife.

Puppy: An alimentary canal with a whine at one end and no sense of responsibility at the other.

Puppy love: The beginning of a dog's life.

Recession: When we do without things our parents never had.

Rich relative: The kind you love to touch.

Rodeo: A show that can have an all-steer cast.

Senator: Half man and half horse.

Sex: Having fun without laughing.

Snoozer: 1/2 poodle and 1/2 schnauzer.

Standing ovation: A hen laying an egg while in a standing position.

Supermarket: Where you spend an hour trying to find instant coffee.

Sycophant: Mentally disturbed pachyderm.

Sympathy: What you give someone when you don't want to lend him money.

Tax accountant: Someone who solves a problem you didn't know you had in a way you don't understand.

Udder Failure: A cow that has gone dry.

Unit of chromosomal circulation: A gene artery.

Vacation: A period when you are cut off from everything familiar—but expenses.

Vet: D.V.M. who was in the war.

Virus: Latin for "Your guess is as good as mine."

Water pollution: Cirrhosis of the river.

Wolf: A big dame hunter.

D.V.M.*
*Department of Veterinary Mirth

Veterinary Definitions by Shakespeare
(assisted by S. Glasofer, D.V.M.)

Two Gentlemen of Verona:

Anomaly: How long hath she been deformed?

Acute hepatitis: With liver burning hot.

Bradycardia: It makes me have a slow heart.

Client's description of patient: My dog be the sourest natured dog that lives; She hath more qualities than a water spaniel; One that I brought up of a puppy.

Consideration of surgical intervention: I have operations in my head.

Surgical anesthesia: Now the dog all this while sheds not a tear nor speaks a word.

Twelfth Night:

Anorexia: The appetite may sicken and so die. Taste with a distempered appetite.

After all-night surgery: By the clock 'tis day and vet dark night strangles the travelling   lamp.

After-hours emergency: To be up after midnight and to go to bed then is early.

Airborne respiratory disease: A contagious breath.

Redundant anamnesis: Enough; no more; 'tis not as sweet now as it was before.

Thrombus: This does make some obstruction in the blood.

Henry V:

Negative prognosis: Nay, 'tis past praying for. There is no remedy; No medicine in the world can do thee good.

Veterinary seminar: A little room confining mighty men.

Merry Wives of Windsor:

Bilateral otic artresia: The ears are senseless that should give us hearing.

Consideration of surgical intervention: I have operations in my head.

Meat inspector: For on his choice depends the safety and health of the whole state.

Unsuccessful case: He is dead and gone, lady. He is dead and gone.

Why I didn't include more: Brevity is the soul of wit.

The Tempest:

Tetany: They grind their joints with dry convulsions: shorten up their sinews with aged cramps.

Hamlet:

Differential diagnosis: What is your cause of distemper?

Negative prognosis: No medicine in the world can do thee good.

Macbeth:

Airborne respiratory disease: Infected be the air whereon they ride.

Experienced surgeon: Such sanctity hath heaven given his hand.

Leukemia: Thy bones are marrowless, thy blood is cold.

Locoweed poisoning: Eaten on the insane root.

Need for a specialist: This disease is beyond my practice.

Otitis treatment: Pour my spirts in thine ear.

Small animal patients: As hounds and greyhounds, mongrels, spaniels, curs, shoughs, water-rugs and demi-wolves are clept all by the name of dogs.

Track veterinarian: I wish your horses swift and sure of foot.

Transfusion: It will have blood; they say, blood will have blood.

Tranquilizer: Balm of hurt mind.

The end: We will proceed no further in this business.

Also available from Lincoln Herndon Press:

Grandpa's Rib-Ticklers and Knee-Slappers*	$ 8.95
Josh Billings—America's Phunniest Phellow*	$ 7.95
Davy Crockett-Legendary Frontier Hero	$ 7.95
Cowboy Life on the Sidetrack	$ 7.95
A Treasury of Science Jokes	$ 9.95
The Great American Liar—Tall Tales	$ 9.95
The Cowboy Humor of A.H. Lewis	$ 9.95
The Fat Mascot — 22 Funny Baseball Stories and More	$ 7.95
A Treasury of Farm and Ranch Humor	$10.95
Mr. Dooley—We Need Him Now!	$ 8.95
A Treasury of Military Humor	$10.95
Here's Charley Weaver, Mamma and Mt. Idy	$ 9.95
A Treasury of Hunting and Fishing Humor	$10.95
A Treasury of Senior Humor	$10.95
A Treasury of Medical Humor	$10.95
A Treasury of Husband and Wife Humor	$10.95
A Treasury of Religious Humor	$10.95
A Treasury of Farm Women's Humor	$12.95
A Treasury of Office Humor	$10.95
A Treasury of Cocktail Humor	$10.95
A Treasury of Business Humor	$12.95
A Treasury of Mom, Pop & Kid's Humor	$12.95
The Humorous Musings of a School Principal	$12.95
A Treasury of Police Humor	$12.95
A Treasury of Veterinary Humor	$12.95

*Available in hardback

The humor in these books will delight you, brighten your conversation, make your life more fun, and healthier, because "Laughter is the Best Medicine."

Order From:
Lincoln-Herndon Press, Inc.
818 South Dirksen Parkway
Springfield, IL 62703
(217) 522-2732
FAX (217)544-8738